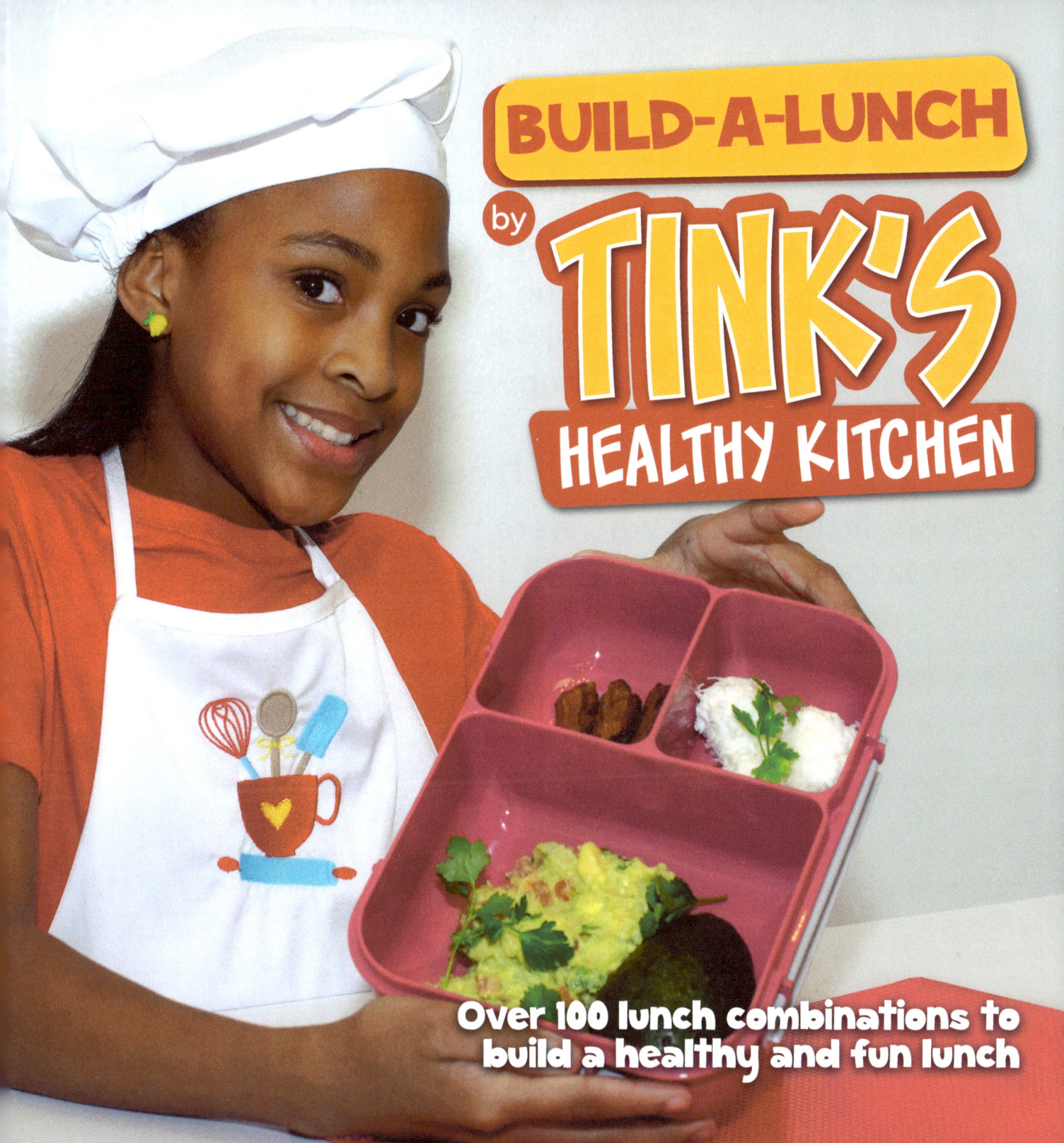

DEDICATION PAGE

To our favorite guys:

Mike *(Dad/Husband)* we appreciate your continued support and for always being our taste tester. To Nahjee *(Brother/Son)* thanks for always encouraging our many business ideas. Together we make a great team!

Special Thanks

To our little friends who were brave enough to try out new foods and gave great feedback: Zayla, Abigal, Kendal and Elaijah. We appreciate your opinions.
Justine Coleman: Our first supporter of
Tink's Organic Lemonade

Acknowledgements

Audrey Hinds: Parker & Co. Press
SaraEllen: J Bella Photography
Frank Pitchford: SoHo Photos
Dave Lentz: Page Designer

MOTHER AND DAUGHTER STORY

Eating healthy does not have to be boring, it can be fun and rewarding. Amanni and I found this out after a doctor's visit and experimenting in the kitchen! Our healthy eating journey began after Amanni was diagnosed with ADHD in the 3rd grade. Before then we lived for eating but we now have learned how to eat to live. After many hours of researching ADHD it was clear that Amanni's sugar intake was one of the biggest disruptors of her attention and behavior. As a family, we decided to remove white granulated sugar from our cabinets. We noticed positive changes right away. Not only did Amanni's behavior improve, but I lost weight with minimal effort. This small change made a huge difference, and we didn't want to stop there. We had discovered a new way to think about eating, and we experimented with new recipes. We set out to prove that Amanni could enjoy the same food without the addictive white sugar.

Amanni was never a fan of school lunches but the lunches we made at home weren't very creative. This book makes it easy for Amanni to pack her lunch and make great food choices. This book will encourage children to try new food and change how they think about healthy food. Making healthy choices can be yummy and fun!

-PAM SPRATLEY

I remember we were in the kitchen trying to re-create one of my favorite drinks, lemonade. We went to the store and bought organic lemons, spring water and different natural sweeteners. Some of the sweeteners were nasty and some were okay. We kept trying to make lemonade with the different ingredients until finally it all came together! I knew we had found "the one" when my dad gave me two thumbs up!

I've learned that choosing healthier food also gives me more energy to enjoy activities. I've become more active. I like running races and I ride my bike every chance I get.

-AMANNI SPRATLEY

We had no intention of selling the lemonade. We wanted family and friends to try our version of a household favorite. Before we knew it, everyone was asking to purchase our lemonade. Since then, we've sold over 1,000 bottles of Tink's Organic Lemonade through word-of-mouth and local vendor events. What we put in our bodies matters to us and we want other children to care about their bodies too. It's been several years since we last purchased a bag of white granulated sugar and we have not looked back. We enjoy food more now than ever!

Happy Eating!

-PAM/AMANNI

www.tinks.healthy.kitchen.com

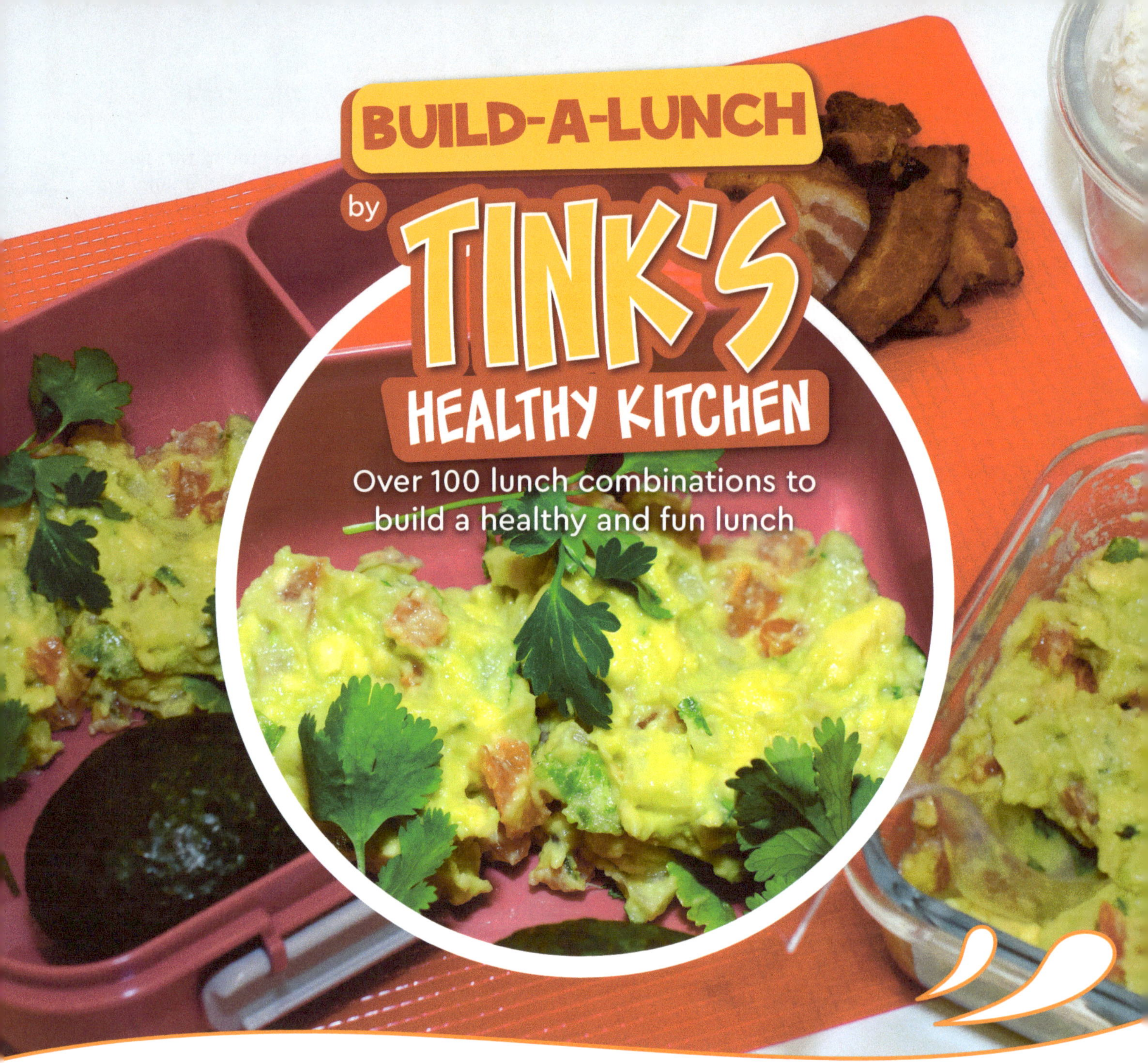

BUILD-A-LUNCH

by

TINK'S HEALTHY KITCHEN

Over 100 lunch combinations to build a healthy and fun lunch

THIS BOOK BELONGS TO

_____

CONTENTS

Recipes

- 5 Subject Taco Dip — 18
- 6-inch Math Sandwich Sticks — 20
- A+ Apple Snail — 60
- Aaliyah's Chicken Friend Cauli-Rice — 22
- Abby's Banana Sushi Rolls — 102
- Archery Salad Cups — 62
- Brandy's Backpack Salad Sticks — 64
- Camilla's Queso Dip — 106
- Cafeteria Chili — 24
- Carley's Cauliflower Popcorn — 66
- Cheeleader Cheese Chips — 104
- Cheese and Bacon Honor Roll Ups — 26
- Cheesy Weezy Quesadilly — 28
- Chelsea's Chick and Waffle Sticks — 30
- Chess Club Cheese Cubes — 108
- Class Pet Orange Snails — 68
- Cool Kid's Chicken Wrap — 32
- Cool Ranch Monster Veggie Cup — 70
- Dolp-Fun Snack Bowls — 72
- Elaijah's Melon Pops — 74
- Field Day Fruit Pizza — 110
- Field Trip Foudue — 112
- Friendship Flower cups — 76
- Graduate Granola Bars — 114
- Gym Time Guac — 78
- Homework Humas and Pita Chips — 80
- Janelle's Fruit Jiggles — 116
- 1-2-3 Lemon Bars — 118
- Kendal's Magical Fruit Wands — 82
- Khari's Cookie Cutter Sandwiches — 34
- Kristy's Crunchy Apple Wedges — 120
- Lyniah's Egg-cellent Muffins — 36
- Monday's Mac and Cheese — 38
- Mr. Bates Seafood Salad — 40
- Mr. Moore's Mini Cheesecake — 122
- Mrs. William's Apple Donuts — 84
- Ms. Ramirez' Churro Almonds — 124
- Nurse Brenda's Bacon Brussles — 86
- Patrick's Loaded Potato — 42
- Pep Rally Pin Wheels — 44
- Preston's PB Cookies — 126
- Raylee's Roasted Chickpeas — 128
- Recess Popcorn Balls — 130
- Riah's Beans and Rice — 46
- Rickey Johnson's Perfect Pasta — 48
- Safety Patrol Peppers — 88
- Skylar's Spinach Dip — 90
- Spotted Butterfly Bites — 132
- Stacy's Salt & Pepper Cucumber Chips — 92
- Sugar Free Science Cookies — 134
- Summer School Bruschetta — 94
- Sweet Potato Lunch Box Crisps — 96
- Teacher's Treat Trail Mix — 136
- Test Day Turkey Burgers — 50
- TGI Fried Green Tomatoes — 98
- Track Team Traveling Nachos — 52
- Valentine's Day Pizza — 54
- Winter Break Snowballs — 138
- Zayla's Chicken Zoodle Soup — 56
- Zihyon's Zucchini Muffins — 140

7 STEPS TO GET A GRADE A+ IN THE KITCHEN!

1. Ask an adult before beginning
2. Wash Hands often
3. Clean as you go
4. Read each recipe twice before starting
5. Come prepared with all ingredients
6. Tie long hair back
7. No horseplaying

HOME EC. TERMS

Al dente- A firm bite/not soft

Blend- Combining two or more ingredients until they become one uniform texture

Chop- Cut food into bite size pieces with knife

Dollop- A small spoonful amount of soft food; typically a topping like whipped cream & sour cream

Grind- To break food down into small pieces (usually with a blender or similar kitchen gadget)

Knead- Work into dough by hand

Marinate- Pre-soak food in a liquid mixture before cooking

Puree'- Cook food until very soft, forming a paste-like consistency

Reduce- Turn back temperature from high to medium or low

Simmer- Cooking hot liquids just below boiling point

Toss Lightly- Combine ingredients using tongs to distribute evenly in a container

Whisk- Mix foods using a whisk which will aerate and increase volume in dish

Zest- Remove outer skin from citrus fruits using a grater, knife or peeler

PRINCIPAL'S MEASURING CHEAT SHEET

SYMBOL KEY

- Teaspon
- 1 Cup
- Tablespoon
- 1 Pint
- 1/4 Cup

3 Teaspoons = 1 Tablespoon

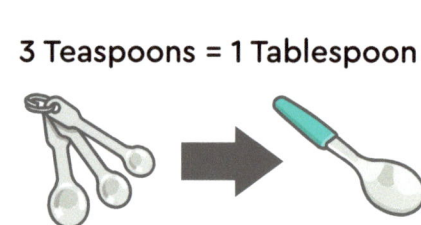

4 Tablespoon = 1/4 cup

16 Tablespoon = 1 cup

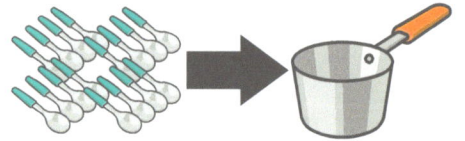

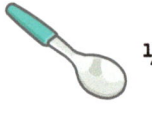 ½ ounce

 2 ounces

 8 ounces OR 1cup

 16 ounces OR 2 cup OR 1pint

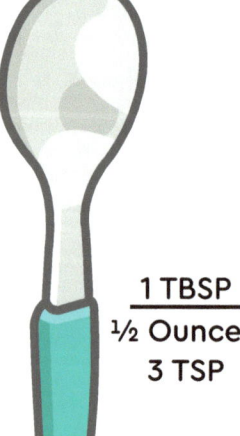

1 TBSP
½ Ounce
3 TSP

1 GALLON
4 QUARTS
8 PINTS
16 CUPS
128 OUNCES

1 QUARTS
2 PINTS
4 CUPS
32 OUNCES

1 PINTS
2 CUPS
16 OUNCES
481 ML

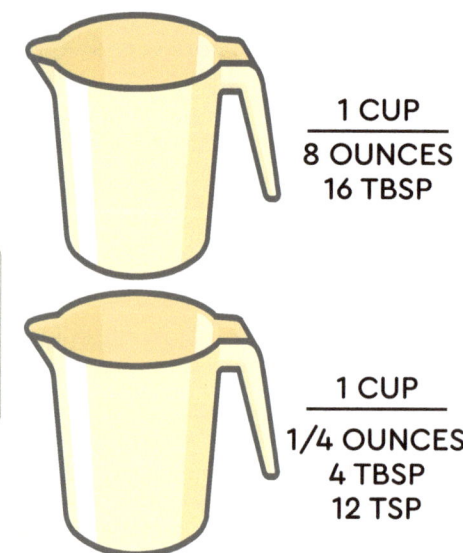

1 CUP
8 OUNCES
16 TBSP

1 CUP
1/4 OUNCES
4 TBSP
12 TSP

KITCHEN TOOLS

KITCHEN TOOLS

Chef Knife Paring Knife Butter Knife

KNIFE SAFETY

- SELECT THE RIGHT KNIFE FOR THE TASK
- KEEP BLADES SHARPENED AND HANDLES IN GOOD CONDITION
- ALWAYS USE A CUTTING BOARD
- CUT DOWNWARDS WITH FIRM EVEN PRESSURE, AWAY FROM THE BODY
- CLEAN KNIVES IMMEDIATELY AFTER USE
- STORE KNIVES SAFELY IN BLOCK OR RACK
- NEVER TRY TO CATCH A FALLING KNIFE

PACKING YOUR BEST LUNCH USING A THERMOS

Caution: Have an Adult Assist You

Heat your thermos by filling it with boiling water. Put the lid on it. Let it sit for 5 minutes then pour out the water. Wipe away any water and then quickly add hot food (at or above 74°C or 165°F) and put the lid on tightly.

Cool your thermos by placing it in the freezer overnight. In most thermoses your food will stay hot or cold for up to 4 hours!

UNDERSTANDING THE COOKBOOK SKILL LEVEL SYMBOL

 **1 hat** indicates a beginner skill level recipe

 **2 hats** indicates a moderate skill level recipe

 **3 hats** indicate an advance skill level recipe

FOOD GROUPS

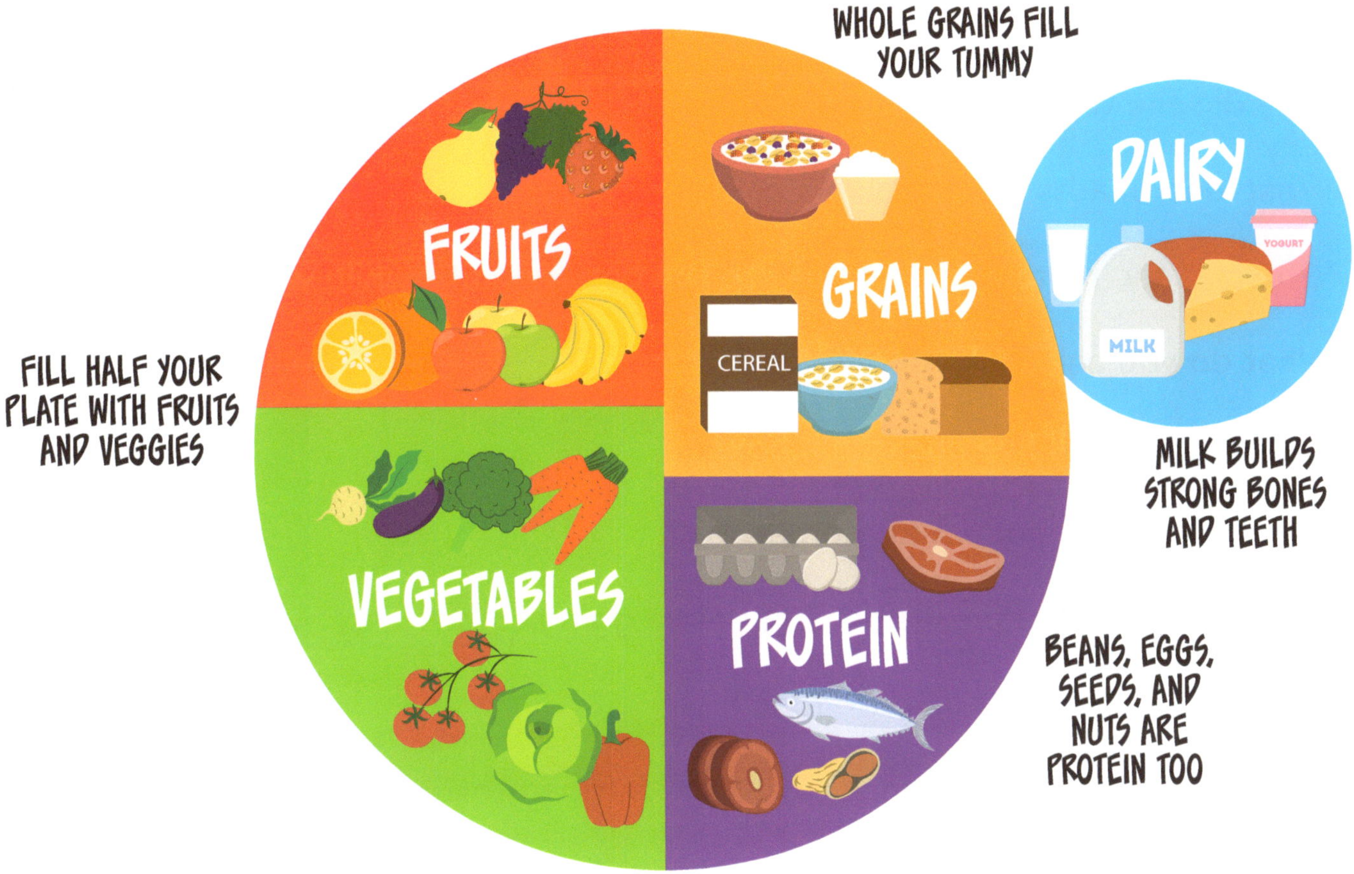
WHOLE GRAINS FILL YOUR TUMMY
FRUITS
GRAINS
DAIRY
YOGURT
MILK
CEREAL
FILL HALF YOUR PLATE WITH FRUITS AND VEGGIES
MILK BUILDS STRONG BONES AND TEETH
VEGETABLES
PROTEIN
BEANS, EGGS, SEEDS, AND NUTS ARE PROTEIN TOO

Doctor's Thoughts

"A body is much like a racecar, what you put in it will determine how it performs."
-Arlene Harrington, MD

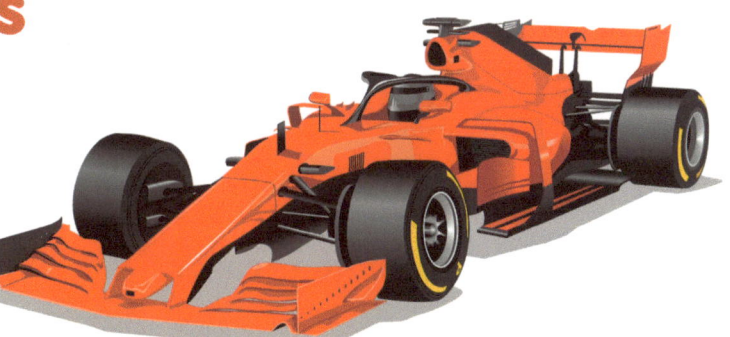

FOOD JOKES

1. Knock, knock. Who's there? Lettuce. Lettuce Who?

2. Why did the tomato blush?

3. What kind of nuts always have a cold?

4. What did the mommy tomato say to the baby tomato while walking?

5. What do you call a fake noodle?

6. What do you call five ducks in a box?

7. Why did the student eat his homework?

8. Customer: "Excuse me waiter is my pizza going to be long?"

9. What's an astronaut's favorite food?

10. What did the bottle of ranch say to the refrigerator?

11. What do you call a granola bar that sneezes?

12. What are twins favorite fruits?

13. Where do burgers go to dance?

14. What did the pecan say to the walnut?

15. What are baby potatoes called?

FOR THE ANSWERS TURN TO PAGE 144

FOOD JOKES

16. Why did the kid run outside with a bowl and spoon?

17. What's a tree's favorite soda?

18. What has a T in the beginning, T in the middle, and a T at the end?

19. Why did the butcher work extra hours at the shop?

20. Why couldn't the sesame seed leave the party?

21. When do you go at red and stop at green?

22. What do you call cheese that is sad?

23. What do call strawberries playing the guitar?

24. What did the hot dog say when his friend passed him in the race?

25. What did the tic tac think of his clothes when he picked them up from the cleaners?

26. What do you get when you play Tug-of-War with a pig?

27. Did you see the movie about the hot dog?

28. What's hard to beat for breakfast?

29. It was an emotional wedding. Why?

30. Why was the soup crying when the toast asked to marry her?

FOR THE ANSWERS TURN TO PAGE 144

ELEMENTARY DISHES

Choose one item from each section to build a well-balanced meal. What creations will you come up with?

In elementary school we learn the importance of eating healthy. We are first introduced to the food pyramid and we begin to understand good food choices versus not so good choices. This section is dedicated to dishes that are main meals. These dishes can be enjoyed alone or paired with food from the other sections. These dishes offer protein, fiber, and carbohydrates.

Turn to page 58 for Secondary Dishes
Turn to page 100 for Graduate Dishes

ELEMENTARY DISHES

- 5 Subject Taco Dip
- 6 inch Math Sandwich Sticks
- Aaliyah's Chicken Fried Cauli Rice
- Cafeteria Chili
- Cheese and Bacon Honor Rollups
- Cheesy Weesy Quesadilly
- Chelsea's Chick and Waffle Sticks
- Cool Kid's Chicken Wrap
- Khari's Cookie Cutter Sandwiches
- Lexi's Egg-cellent Muffins
- Monday's Mac & Cheese Cups
- Mr. Bates seafood salad
- Patrick's Loaded Potato
- Pep Rally Pinwheels
- Riah's Beans and Rice
- Rickey Johnson's Perfect Pasta
- Test Day Turkey Burgers
- Track Team Traveling Nachos
- Valentine's Day Pizza
- Zayla's Chicken Zoodle Soup

5 Subject Taco Dip

Prep Time: 10 min

Difficulty:

Equipment Needed:

Small Container with Lid

Spoon

Ingredients:

¼ cup sour cream

2 ounces cream cheese

½ pack of taco seasoning

½ cup shredded cheddar cheese

½ cup salsa

½ cup shredded lettuce

Optional: jalapenos & olives

Instructions

1. Mix cream cheese, sour cream and taco seasoning
2. Add a layer to the bottom of your container
3. Spread layer two (Sala over your mixture)
4. Next is layer 3 – shredded cheese
5. Layer 4 – Shredded lettuce
6. Repeat layers if you choose
7. Top with jalapenos or olives
8. Enjoy with tortillas!

6 INCH MATH SANDWICHES

Prep Time: 5 min

Difficulty: 🎓

Equipment Needed:
Wooden Diol or Skewer
Parchment Paper

Ingredients:
You chose!
Here's where you have total control
What's in your fridge?
Build your wildest creation

Instructions
1. Cut all food items into 2 to 4-inch bites
2. Build sandwich on the stick leaving room to hold on each end
3. Pack favorite dressing dipping
4. Enjoy!

AALIYAH'S CHICKEN FRIED CAULI-RICE

Prep Time: 10 min
Cooking Time: 20 min

Equipment Needed:
Small bowl
Medium skillet
Mixing spoon

Ingredients:
3 ounces skinless boneless chicken breast; cut into small pieces
1 tablespoon soy sauce
1 tablespoon apple vinegar
½ tablespoon cornstarch
2 ½ tablespoons vegetable oil - divided
½ cup broccoli; cut into pieces
¼ cup green pepper; cut into squares
¼ cup carrots cubed
1 tablespoon minced garlic
¼ cup chicken broth
3 green onion chopped
1 cup frozen cooked cauliflower rice
optional mushrooms

Difficulty: 🎓🎓🎓

Instructions

1. Preheat cauliflower rice; set aside
2. Mix chicken, soy sauce, vinegar, cornstarch together; set aside
3. Heat vegetable oil in skillet on medium high; add veggies and garlic; simmer for 3 minutes; add chicken broth, cover and simmer for 4 minutes (until veggies are tender); transfer to bowl
4. Wipe pan clean; add 2 tsp vegetable oil on medium heat; add chicken; stir until center in no longer pink, approx. 5 mins; add vegetables; continue to cook for an additional 3 minutes; top with green onion
5. Reduce heat to low; add rice and mix
6. Enjoy in warm thermos!

CAFETERIA CHILI

Prep Time: 5 min
Cooking Time: 25 min

Difficulty:

Equipment Needed:
Small frying pan
Medium Saucepan
Wooden Spoon
Strainer
Knife for chopping

Ingredients:
½ tablespoon olive oil
½ cup chicken broth
¼ pound ground turkey
¼ cup chopped onion
¼ cup chopped green pepper
2 tablespoons chili powder
1 tablespoon chopped garlic
½ cup (undrained) canned diced tomatoes
¼ cup drained kidney beans
Salt and Pepper to taste

Instructions

1. Heat olive oil in frying pan, add turkey and cook over medium heat, stir often and cook for 5 minutes until meat browns (be sure to break up any clumps)
2. Drain meat in strainer; set aside
3. Place saucepan on stove on medium heat
4. Add onion, green pepper, chili powder, garlic and cook for 5 minutes to allow the vegetables to cook down
5. Add turkey to pot mixture and stir
6. Add tomatoes, salt and pepper and chicken broth; bring to a boil
7. Reduce heat, simmer stir occasionally and allow chili to cook for another 15 minutes
8. Enjoy in warm thermos!

CHEESE AND BACON HONOR-ROLL UPS

Prep Time: 5 min
Cooking Time: 6 min

Difficulty:

Equipment Needed:

Tongs
Small frying pan
Rolling Pin

Ingredients:

2 slices of bread (crust removed)
2 slices of cheese
2 slices of pre-cooked bacon
2 tablespoons butter

Instructions

1. Using rolling pin flatten bread
2. Place cheese on bread and roll up
3. Wrap bacon around roll up
4. Add butter to pan / heat on low temperature
5. Cook 2 mins turning on each side with tongs until cheese is melted
6. Remove from heat and pat with paper towel to dry
7. Enjoy in warm thermos!

CHEESY WEEZY QUESADILLY

Prep Time: 15 min
Cooking Time: 10 min

Difficulty: 🎓🎓

Equipment Needed:
Medium size skillet
Spatula
Pizza cutter
Large plate

Ingredients:
2 Flour Tortillas
1 cup cheese
(½ cheddar and ½ mozzarella works well)
1 tablespoon butter

Instructions
1. Melt ½ of the butter in the skillet
2. Fry one side of first tortilla for 2 minutes; remove from pan
3. Melt the other ½ of butter in skillet; fry second tortilla (leave in pan), Sprinkle cheese evenly around tortilla; Top with your 1st tortilla
4. Press tortillas firmly together with a spatula until the cheese is melted
5. Remove from pan and use pizza cutter to cut triangle wedges
6. Enjoy in warm thermos!

These can be stacked in a sandwich holder or wrapped in foil for easy lunch box packing

*For added flavor; add meat or peppers

*Also enjoy with a side of salsa and sour cream

CHELSEA'S CHICKEN AND WAFFLE STICKS

Prep Time: 10 min
Cooking Time: 5 min

Difficulty:

Equipment Needed:
Skewers

Ingredients:
2 pre-cooked chicken tenders
4 mini waffles
2 tablespoons sugar-free syrup

Instructions
1. Cut heated chicken tenders into chunks
2. Toast mini waffles; pull apart
3. Starting with the chicken stack the chicken and waffles onto the skewer saving space for holding
4. Using a small container; pack your sugar-free syrup for dipping
5. Enjoy in warm thermos!

*Instead of dipping syrup, add fruit to your skewers. Blueberries and Strawberries work well!

COOL KID'S CHICKEN WRAP

Prep Time: 15 min

Difficulty: 🎓🎓

Equipment Needed:
Medium mixing bowl
Mixing spoon
Measuring spoon
Parchment paper
Butter knife

Ingredients:
½ cup canned chicken breast chopped
Dash of salt
Dash of ground black pepper
2 tablespoons mayo
½ teaspoon lemon juice
½ stalk celery chopped finely
Thin slice lunchmeat
2 teaspoons ranch salad dressing
Whole wheat tortilla
Shredded lettuce
Diced Tomatoes

Instructions
1. Mix the first 6 ingredients together in a medium mixing bowl, set aside
2. Lay tortilla down on parchment paper
3. With butter knife spread ranch dressing in center of tortilla
4. Add lunch meat
5. Add two scoops of chicken salad to middle of tortilla
6. Add shredded lettuce and diced tomatoes
7. To wrap; fold sides in first, then bring up top and bottom flaps and continue to roll
8. Cut in half for easy packing and holding
9. Enjoy!

KHARI'S COOKIE CUTTER SANDWICHES

Prep Time: 5 min

Difficulty:

Equipment Needed:
Parchment Paper
Butter Knife
Cookie Cutters

Ingredients:
2 slices whole wheat bread
1 slice lunch meat
1 slice cheese
(optional mayo or mustard)

Instructions
1. Build your normal sandwich
2. Using your cookie cutter cut sandwiches into desired shapes
3. Enjoy!

LYNIAH'S EGG-CELLENT MUFFINS

Prep Time: 10 min
Cooking Time: 25 min

Difficulty: 🎓🎓🎓

Equipment Needed:
Muffin Pan
Small skillet
Whisk
Small bowl
Mixing Bowl

Ingredients:
Cooking spray
2 precooked bacon strips cut up
3 large eggs
½ cup chopped spinach
¼ cup mozzarella cheese
¼ chopped small yellow onion
2 teaspoons milk
¼ teaspoon garlic powder
1/8 teaspoon paprika
Salt and Pepper to taste

Instructions

1. Preheat oven to 350 F
2. Line 4 Muffin cups with nonstick cooking spray; add 1 Tablespoon water in unused cups
3. In skillet cook onion until it's translucent; set aside
4. In small bowl whisk eggs, milk, garlic powder, paprika, salt and pepper
5. Add onion, bacon, spinach and mozzarella cheese to bowl
6. Pour egg evenly into muffin cups, Bake until golden brown 25-30 minutes
7. Enjoy in warm thermos!

MONDAY'S MAC AND CHEESE CUPS

Prep Time: 10 min
Cooking Time: 20 min

Difficulty: 🎓🎓🎓

Equipment Needed:
Medium Pot
Muffin Pan
Colander
Mixing Spoon
Lg Spoon for scooping

Ingredients:
¼ cup elbow macaroni
4 ounces shredded sharp cheese
1 teaspoon butter
1 teaspoon four
1/8 cup milk
Nonstick cooking spray

Instructions
1. Preheat oven to 400 degrees F
2. Place 6 cupcake liners in muffin pan, spray each with nonstick cooking spray
3. On top of stove; Cook pasta according to box (Do not cook for more than 8 minutes)
4. Drain pasta in colander, set aside
   wipe some starch from pan with paper towel
5. On medium high; add butter to pot, mix until melted, slowly add flour and stir for 2 minutes
6. Once butter and flour have blended slowly pour in milk; bring to a boil
7. Add shredded cheese; reducing heat to low, allow cheese to completely melt
8. Stir until you have a smooth cheese sauce consistency; add pasta to mix, being sure to coat all pasta; remove from heat
9. Using a spoon, place portions of mac and cheese into each muffin cup
10. Add additional cheese to the top of each muffin before baking; Bake for 8-10 minutes
11. Remove from oven and immediately add to thermos, enjoy!

MR. BATE'S SEAFOOD SALAD

Prep Time: 15 min
Cooking Time: Pasta cooking time 8 min

Difficulty:

Equipment Needed:
Medium mixing bowl
Mixing spoon
Measuring spoons
Colander

Ingredients:
¼ cup al dente cooked seashell pasta noodles
½ cup crabmeat or imitation crabmeat
2 ounces salad shrimp
½ chopped celery stalk
2 tablespoons mayonnaise
¼ pinch paprika
¼ teaspoon black pepper
¼ teaspoon seafood seasoning (Old Bay™)
½ teaspoon dried parsley

Instructions
1. Cook pasta according to package
2. Dump pasta into colander, run cool water over and set aside
3. Mix all other ingredients together
4. Add cool pasta to salad mix
5. Mix all ingredients well
6. Refrigerate until ready to pack for lunch
7. Enjoy in chilled thermos!

PATRICK'S LOADED POTATO

Prep Time: 5 min
Cooking time: 10 min

Difficulty:

Equipment Needed:
Fork
Plastic Sandwich Bag
Small microwavable plate
Butter Knife

Ingredients:
1 small Russet potato - washed
1 tablespoon butter
2 tablespoons cheese
Salt to taste
1 teaspoon sour cream
Bacon Bits

Instructions
1. Pierce the potato with a fork; place in sandwich bag and on plate
2. Microwave potato for 5-7 minutes depending on size and microwave power
3. Remove from microwave, carefully remove from plastic bag. Cut down center
4. Add butter and salt to the center of potato, top with cheese
5. Replace potato in microwave on plate (not in bag), microwave for 1-3 minutes
6. Remove from microwave and place immediately in thermos.
7. Top with sour cream and bacon bits
8. Enjoy in warm thermos!

PEP RALLY PIN WHEELS

Prep Time: 10 min

Difficulty:

Equipment Needed:
Medium mixing bowl
Mixing spoon
Cutting Knife

Ingredients:
1 4 ounces cup of pre-cooked chicken breast
1/4 cup nonfat plain Greek yogurt
½ tbsp Dijon mustard
½ chopped celery stalk *optional*
cracked pepper and salt to taste
1 medium size tortilla

Instructions
1. In a medium bowl mix chicken breast and Greek yogurt
2. Add Dijon mustard and celery
3. Add salt and pepper to taste
4. Stir ingredients; refrigerate for 1 hr. to allow ingredients to settle well
5. Add finished salad to tortilla, roll and cut into wheels
6. Enjoy chilled!
- For added flavor add nuts and grapes

RIAH'S BEANS AND RICE

Prep Time: 5 min
Cooking Time: 30 min

Difficulty: 🎓🎓🎓

Equipment Needed:
Saucepan
Wooden Spoon
Knife for cutting

Ingredients:
¼ cup cooked rice
¼ cup andouille sausage; thinly sliced
½ small diced onion
½ chopped green bell pepper
½ 6 ounce can tomato paste
1 teaspoon minced garlic
1 cup chicken broth
1 bay leaf
1 15 ounce red beans drained and rinsed
Salt and Pepper to taste

Instructions

1. Cook rice according to package; set aside
2. In a saucepan cook sausage until browned on both sides (4mins)
3. Add onions and bell peppers; cook until tender (3 mins)
4. Stir in tomato paste and garlic
5. Add v, chicken broth, bay leaf; bring to a boil
6. Remove ¼ cp beans, mash completely the add back into pot
7. Season with salt and pepper to taste
8. Cover and reduce heat – simmer for 20 mins
9. Enjoy in warm thermos!

RICKEY JOHNSON'S PERFECT PASTA

Prep Time: 15 min
Cooking Time: 8 min

Difficulty: 🎓🎓

Equipment Needed:

Measuring Cup and Large Mixing Spoon
Safe Cutting Knife and Cutting Board
4 Quart Pot
Colander
Measuring spoons
1 medium salad bowl
1 small bowl

Ingredients:

¼ medium red onion, diced
¼ green bell pepper, diced
½ cup Zesty Italian Dressing
4 ounces Rainbow Rotini Pasta
4 ounces Diced Tomatoes
½ small cucumber, sliced and quartered
1 tablespoon Salad Supreme seasoning ™

Instructions

1. Add onion, pepper and Italian dressing to the small bowl, mix, and place to the side to marinate
2. Cook pasta according to package
3. Remove pasta, rinse under cool water and drain in colander
4. Place well-drained pasta and salad ingredients into a medium bowl and mix well, add marinate mix with pasta
5. Chill pasta salad for at least 30 minutes before serving to allow flavors to blend
6. Enjoy chilled or at room temperature!

TEST-DAY TURKEY BURGERS

Prep Time: 15 min
Cooking Time: 20 min

Difficulty: 🎓🎓🎓

Equipment Needed:
Medium bowl
Mixing spoon
Muffin Pan
Meat thermometer

Ingredients:
¼ pound ground turkey
2 tablespoons chopped parsley
1 dash cumin
¼ teaspoon smoked paprika
¼ teaspoon cracked pepper
½ teaspoon garlic salt
4 slider buns
*options cheese slices

Instructions

1. Preheat oven to 350 F
2. Mix v, parsley, cumin, paprika , garlic salt, and cracked pepper in bowl, form 4 small patties
3. Place patties in muffin cup and bake for 15-20 minutes, inside temperature of each burger should be 165 degrees
4. Remove from oven and allow to cool before handling
5. Build each burger in pre-warmed thermos to keep warm!
6. Enjoy!

TRACK TEAM TRAVELING NACHOS

Prep Time: 5 min
Cooking time: 10 min

Difficulty: 🎓🎓

Equipment Needed:

Medium Skillet

Spoon

Ingredients:

¼ pound ground beef

1 tablespoon taco seasoning

¼ cup shredded lettuce

1 2.5 ounces bag nacho v

1 tablespoon chopped tomato

¼ cup shredded cheddar cheese

¼ cup water

Instructions

1. Place ground beef in a medium skillet. Cook and stir over medium heat until browned. Drain excess oil. Mix in the taco seasoning and water. Store in thermos.
2. At lunch, open bag completely, spoon in beef over chips and top with lettuce, tomatoes and cheese.
3. Enjoy!

VALENTINE'S DAY PIZZA

Prep Time: 10 min
Cooking Time: 15 min

Difficulty:

Equipment Needed:
Muffin pan
Nonstick Cooking Spray
Dipping Spoon
Glass Cup
Heart-Shaped Cookie Cutter

Ingredients:
1 can Crescent Rolls
½ cup mozzarella cheese
¼ cup pizza sauce
¼ cup chopped veggies
8-10 Pepperoni

Instructions

1. Preheat oven 375F
2. Spray muffin pan with non-stick cooking spray
3. Lay crescent rolls out and cut with opening of glass cup; using cookie cutter cut pepperoni
4. Press each circled cutout into a muffin cup
5. Divide vegetables into each pizza cup; Add a spoonful of pizza sauce, Top with mozzarella cheese and pepperoni
6. Bake for 15 min; remove from oven, wait 2 mins before removing from muffin cups
7. Enjoy at room temperature or in warm thermos!

ZAYLA'S CHICKEN ZOODLE SOUP

Prep Time: 5 min
Cooking time: 30-35 min

Difficulty: 🎓🎓🎓

Equipment Needed:

Medium pot

Large mixing Spoon

Ingredients:

1 cp diced cooked chicken breast

1 cup frozen zucchini noodles

½ chopped celery stick

½ small onion, diced finely

¼ cup chopped carrots

1 8oz can chicken broth

1 package dry onion soup

2 cups water

1 teaspoon salt

1 teaspoon garlic powder

Instructions

1. Combine all ingredients except zucchini in medium pot, bring to a boil. Cover and cook over medium heat for 15 minutes
2. Add zucchini to pot, lower heat, cook for additional 20 mins
3. Allow to cool before enjoying in a warm thermos!

SECONDARY DISHES

As we start to understand the importance of food, we begin to make better choices. This section of food is just that; "the better for you dishes". Included are lots of delicious fruits and vegetables. Feel free to try one or two at a time! There's no such thing as too many here.

SECONDARY DISHES

- A+ Apple Snail
- Archery Salad Cup
- Brandy's Backpack Salad Sticks
- Carley's Cauliflower Popcorn
- Class Pet Orange Snails
- Cool Ranch Monster Veggie Cup
- Dolp-fun Snack Bowls
- Elaijah's Watermelon Pops
- Friendship Flower Cups
- Gym Time Guac
- Homework Hummus and Pita Chips
- Kendal's Magical Fruit Wands
- Mrs. William's Apple Donuts
- Nurse Brenda's Bacon Brussels
- Safety Patrol Peppers
- Skylar's Spinach Dip
- Stacy's Salt and Vinegar Cucumber Chips
- Summer School Bruschetta
- Sweet Potato Lunch Box Crisps
- TGI Fried Green Tomatoes

A+ APPLE SNAIL

Prep Time: 7 min

Difficulty:

Equipment Needed:
Knife for cutting
Sandwich bag
Scissors

Ingredients:
Washed and dried small apple
2 tablespoons peanut butter
semi-sweet chocolate morsel
celery hearts
1 part water / 1 part lemon mix
Pretzels Sticks

Instructions
1. Cut apple into thin wedge slices; emerge into lemon mix
2. Emerge slices into lemon mix
3. Spoon peanut butter into corner of sandwich bag; cut small hole for squeezing
4. Squeeze a line of peanut butter onto the center of celery
5. Add apple slice; chocolate morsels for eyes and pretzel sticks for antennas as shown
6. Store each snail side by side in an airtight container
7. Enjoy!

ARCHERY SALAD CUPS

Prep Time: 10 min **Difficulty:**

Equipment Needed:
Plastic cup with lid
Cutting Knife

Ingredients:
¼ cup shredded lettuce
¼ cup shredded red cabbage
¼ cup shredded carrots
4-5 cherry tomatoes
5 slices diced cucumbers
chopped onion to taste
chopped peppers to taste
optional bacon bits
2 teaspoons favorite dressing

Instructions
1. In a plastic cup pour 2 TSP dressing
2. Build your salad one ingredient at a time
3. Place lid to secure cup
4. When ready to enjoy, remove all ingredients and mix well.
5. Enjoy chilled!

BRANDY'S BACKPACK SALAD ON A STICK

Prep Time: 5-7 min

Difficulty: 🎓

Equipment Needed:
Knife for cutting
Boiled Wooden Skewers

Ingredients:
Fresh washed and dried vegetables
Cherry Tomatoes
Romaine Lettuce
Chunky cut onions
Pre-cooked bacon strips
Blue Cheese Crumbles
Ranch Dressing

Instructions
1. Build each skewer according to your liking
2. Secure each skewer at the top with a tomato
3. Pack blue cheese crumbles and dressing
4. When ready to enjoy drizzle crumbles and dressing over each stick!

CARLEY'S CAULIFLOWER POPCORN

Prep Time: 5 min
Cooking time: 20-25 min

Difficulty: 🎓🎓🎓

Equipment Needed:
Small Bowl
Parchment Paper
Cookie Sheet
Knife for cutting

Ingredients:
1 cup cauliflower florets
Parmesan popcorn salt
1 Tablespoon Olive Oil

Instructions

1. Preheat oven to 400 F
2. Mix olive oil & parmesan salt in bowl (being sure not to over salt)
3. Add cauliflower florets; cover and shake bowl to coat completely
4. On parchment covered cookie sheet dump cauliflower
5. Bake 15-20 minutes
6. For fun pack cauliflower in popcorn container or enjoy in warm thermos!

CLASS PET ORANGE SNAILS

Prep Time: 5 min

Difficulty:

Equipment Needed:
Small paring knife
Scissors

Ingredients:
Small Naval Orange
Parchment Paper

Instructions
1. Gather your washed and dried naval orange and place on a sheet of parchment paper
2. Cut all but 1 5-inch strip from the orange being sure not to puncture through the outer wall to expose juice
3. Cut two ear-shaped part to the top of your exposed strip
4. Using a marker, draw eyes and mouth to your snail
5. Enjoy!

COOL RANCH MONSTER VEGGIE CUP

Prep Time: 5 min

Difficulty:

Equipment Needed:
Knife for cutting

Ingredients:
Clean and dried vegetables
3 Bell Peppers of your choice
¼ cup ranch dressing
One olive sliced in half
Dollop of cream cheese

Instructions
1. Cut the top of one pepper: cleaning out seeds from the inside forming a pepper cup. Rinse and set aside to dry
2. Using the remainder peppers; cut each into strips
3. Pour ranch into bottom of pepper cup
4. Add pepper strips to cup
5. Using cream cheese secure sliced olive to front of pepper to create an eye, secure with toothpick
6. Wrap with foil for transporting
7. Enjoy!

DOLP-FUN SNACK BOWLS

Prep Time: 5 min

Difficulty:

Equipment Needed:

Container

Water Dropper or Spoon

Black Marker

Ingredients:

Fruit washed and dried

Banana cut in half

Grapes (your preference)

1 part water 1 part lemon juice mix

Instructions

1. Fill bottom of container with grapes
2. Dip cut ends of banana into lemon mixture
3. Slit the top half of banana to form a dolphin mouth
4. Using a dropper squeeze lemon mixture into the mouth of the dolphin to prevent browning
5. Using the marker Draw eyes
6. Cover with Saran Wrap for storing and transporting
7. Enjoy!

ELAIJAH'S WATERMELON POP

Prep Time: 10 min **Difficulty:** 🎓

Equipment Needed:
Sharp Knife
Craft Sticks

Ingredients:
small watermelon
(optional salt/cayenne pepper)

Instructions

1. Slice watermelon to one-inch slices
2. Cut each watermelon slice into fourths.
3. Using a knife, cut a small slit in the center of each green rind. (You only want to cut as deep as the green rind)
4. Stick a large craft stick through each slit and push up through the watermelon (Sprinkle optional salt and/or cayenne pepper to taste)
5. Enjoy!

FRIENDSHIP FLOWER CUPS

Prep Time: 10 min

Difficulty:

Equipment Needed:
Toothpicks
Cupcake cup holders
Small flower cookie cutter
Cutting Knife

Ingredients:
Cantaloupe
Green grapes

Instructions

Fresh cleaned dry fruit

1. Slice cantaloupe to ½ inch slices
2. Using cookie cutter punch 5 flowers; insert toothpick and two grapes on the end
3. Place flower in 2 layer cupcake cup holders
4. Store in cold thermos

GYM TIME GUAC

Prep Time: 10 min

Difficulty:

Equipment Needed:
Medium Bowl
Cutting Knife
Masher
Lg. Spoon

Ingredients:
2 medium avocadoes
½ of a lime (juiced)
1 small Roma tomato (center & seeds removed)
¼ cubed red onion
1 teaspoon garlic
1 ½ teaspoon kosher salt

Instructions
1. Cut avocado in halves into a medium size bowl
2. Mash the avocado until it's the consistency of mashed potatoes; add the lime juice and mix
3. Cut Roma tomatoes into small cubes; stir into avocado mix
4. Add cilantro, garlic onions and kosher salt to avocado mix
5. Place in airtight container and place in fridge for 1 hour for full flavor
6. Enjoy chilled or at room temperature!

*Dipping Option: Bacon chips or Cheese chips
(Recipe found in section 2 – pairings)

HOMEWORK HUMMUS AND PITA CHIPS

Prep Time: 10 min

Difficulty: 🎓

Equipment Needed:
Food processor or blender

Ingredients:
½ can chickpeas
¼ cup of warm water
2 tablespoons peanut butter
1 tablespoon olive oil
2 tablespoons lemon juice
Dash of garlic salt to taste

Instructions
1. Add all ingredients to the food processor
2. Blend until you have a smooth consistency
3. Add 1 tbsp of water to loosen the thickness
4. Store in fridge until ready to pack
5. Serve with Pita chips
6. Enjoy chilled or at room temperature!

*Switch it up and dip with celery sticks, carrots, pretzel sticks or croutons!

KENDAL'S MAGICAL FRUIT WANDS

Prep Time: 10 min

Difficulty: 🎓

Equipment Needed:
Large Pot
Wooden Skewers
Cutting Knife
Star Cookie Cutter

Ingredients:
(Washed Fruit)
Sliced and cut watermelon
Cubed cantaloupe
Strawberries (Stems removed)
Blueberries
Grapes

Instructions
1. Pre-Boil wooden skewers in pot to prevent splintering
2. Build each wand (leaving space for holding)
3. Add the fruit (leaving watermelon for top) in any order that you prefer
4. Cut watermelon with star cookie cutter and add to the top of your wand
5. Wands are best packed wrapped in Saran Wrap
6. Enjoy!

Mrs. William's Apple Donuts

Prep Time: 10 min

Difficulty: 🎓

Equipment Needed:
Knife for cutting
Parchment paper

Ingredients:
1 apple sliced ½ inch thick
almond or peanut butter
Toppings of your choice
1 part water / 1 part lemon juice

Instructions
1. Emerge each apple slice into the lemon mix
2. Pat dry
3. Spread almond or peanut butter over one side of each apple slice
4. Add topping
5. Store in airtight container
6. Enjoy!

NURSE BRENDA'S BACON BRUSSELS

Prep Time: 5 min
Cooking time: 20-25 min

Difficulty: 🎓🎓

Equipment Needed:
Parchment Paper
Paper Towel
Cookie Sheet
Toothpick

Ingredients:
4 Thick Slices Bacon
4 Brussels Sprouts
Sugar-Free Maple Syrup

Instructions

1. Preheat oven 350 F
2. Place bacon strips side by side on parchment paper
3. Lightly drizzle sugar free maple syrup over each strip of bacon
4. Add sprouts at the bottom of bacon and roll until reaching the top; secure each with toothpick
5. Place each roll 1 inch a part onto cookie sheet; bake for 20-25 minutes (when bacon is thoroughly cooked)
6. Remove from oven and place rolls on paper towel to dry
7. Enjoy in warm thermos!

SAFETY PATROL PEPPERS

Prep Time: 5 min

Difficulty:

Equipment Needed:

Knife for cutting

Toothpick

Spoon

Small circle cookie cutter

Ingredients:

Clean and dried: Red, Yellow, Green Bell Peppers

1 celery heart

2 teaspoon cream cheese

Instructions

1. Cut celery in half
2. Spoon 1 teaspoon of cream cheese in center of celery
3. Top with cookie-cut pieces of pepper to form stop sign
4. Secure each celery stalk with a toothpick
5. Enjoy!

SKYLAR'S SPINACH DIP

Prep Time: 10 min
Cooking time: 15 min

Difficulty: 🎓🎓

Equipment Needed:
Medium Bowl
Mixing spoon

Ingredients:
5 ounces frozen chopped spinach (thawed and drained)
1 tablespoon melted butter
½ cup grated parmesan cheese
2 ounces sour cream
2 ounces cream cheese (softened)
¼ ounce mozzarella cheese

Instructions

1. Preheat Oven to 350
2. Mix all ingredients in bowl; spread into an 8-inch baking dish; bake 15 min (or until cheese is bubbling)
3. Pack in warmed thermos to keep warm

STACY'S SALT AND VINEGAR CUCUMBER CHIPS

Prep Time: 5 min

Difficulty: 🎓

Equipment Needed:
Knife for cutting
Small bowl with lid

Ingredients:
½ medium cucumber
⅛ cup cool water
¼ cup apple cider vinegar
salt and pepper to taste

Instructions
1. In a small bowl add sliced peeled cucumber ¼ inch thick
2. Mix water and vinegar in bowl; Add salt and pepper to taste
3. Store in a leak proof container for transporting
4. Refrigerate overnight
5. Enjoy in chilled thermos!

SUMMER SCHOOL BRUSCHETTA

Prep Time: 15 min
Cooking time: 5 min

Difficulty:

Equipment Needed:
Cutting knife
Cutting board
Small bowl

Ingredients:
¼ cup Petite Tomatoes
1 tablespoon chopped basil
Salt/Pepper to taste
4 slices of baguette, cut into ½-inch thick
1 tablespoon olive oil

Instructions
1. Cut tomatoes into halves
2. Add tomatoes and basil in bowl and sprinkle salt and pepper
3. Preheat broiler, place baguette slices on baking sheet and broil for 1-2 minutes on each side
4. Remove from broiler and brush each side with olive oil, spoon tomato mixture over bread
5. Pack and Enjoy

Sweet Potato Lunch Box Crisp

Prep Time: 10 min
Cooking time: 50-60 min

Difficulty: 🎓🎓

Equipment Needed:
Cooking Sheet
Spatula
Parchment Paper
Potato Slicer

Ingredients:
1 large sweet potato
Cooking Spray
Cinnamon
Salt to taste

Instructions
1. Scrub and wash sweet potato
2. Preheat oven to 350 F
3. Slice potato into thin slices (for safety use a potato slicer)
4. Soak potatoes in warm water for 10 minutes
5. Line cookie sheet with parchment paper; spray a coat cooking spray
6. Line the cookie sheet in a single layer leaving at least 1 inch apart; sprinkle cinnamon
7. Bake Chips for 25 minutes, flip on opposite side and bake for an additional 25 minutes
8. Super thin chips will bake quick and so watch for crispiness and remove when ready
9. Top with sprinkled salt and enjoy!

TGI-FRIED GREEN TOMATOES

Prep Time: 5 min
Cooking time: 10 min

Difficulty: 🎓🎓

Equipment Needed:
Parchment Paper
2 Small Bowls
Baking Sheet
Tongs

Ingredients:
Firm Green Tomatoes
¼ cup Plain Panko Crust
¼ cup Unsweetened Almond Milk

Instructions
1. Preheat oven to 425 degrees
2. Place panko crust and almond milk in separate bowls
3. Slice tomatoes ¼ inch thick and place on parchment paper
4. Dip each tomato slice in the milk then panko mix being sure to cover both sides evenly
5. Place on baking sheet; bake for 10 mins
6. Using tongs, remove tomatoes
7. Enjoy in warm thermos!

GRADUATE DISHES

As we grow and go our taste buds change with us. This section is dedicated to exploring new dishes. The items found here may be old to some or new to others, but they are fun for all! Take your taste buds on a field trip you'll want to revisit over and over again!

Many of these recipes can be made the night before and enjoyed the next day at lunch!

GRADUATE DISHES

- Abby's Banana Sushi Rolls
- 1-2-3 Lemon Bars
- Camilla's Queso Dip
- Cheerleader Cheese Chips
- Chess Club Cheese Cubes
- Field Day Fruit Pizza
- Field Trip Fondue
- Graduate Granola Bars
- Jeremy's Fruit Jiggles
- Kristy's Crunchy Apple Wedge
- Mr. Moore's Mini Cheesecake
- Ms. Ramirez' Churro Almonds
- Preston's PB Cookies
- Raylee's Roasted Chickpeas
- Recess Popcorn Balls
- Spotted Butterfly Bites
- Sugar Free Science Cookies
- Teacher's Treat Trail Mix
- Winter Break Snowballs
- Zihyon's Zucchini Muffins

ABBY'S BANANA SUSHI ROLLS

Prep Time: 5 min

Difficulty:

Equipment Needed:

Butter knife

Ingredients:

1 medium banana

2 tablespoons peanut butter

1 tablespoon hazelnut spread

1 whole wheat flour tortilla

1 teaspoon lemon juice

Instructions

1. Spread peanut butter onto center of tortilla
2. Add hazelnut atop
3. Follow with banana to center of tortilla
4. Roll tortilla tightly
5. Slice into rolls
6. Place in airtight container
7. Enjoy chilled or at room temperature!

*To avoid bananas browning; drizzle lemon juice over sushi slices before packing

CHEERLEADER CHEESE CHIPS

Prep Time: 5 min
Cooking time: 7 min

Difficulty:

Equipment Needed:
Small bowl
Cookie sheet

Ingredients:
½ cup cheddar cheese
Cooking spray

Instructions

1. Preheat over 400 F
2. Spray cookie sheet with cooking spray
3. Place 1 handful of cheese 5 inches apart from the next onto cookie sheet until your cheese bowl is empty
4. Bake for 6-8 minutes, until cheese begins to bubble
5. Remove from oven; allow time to cool and crisp
6. Transfer from pan to paper towel; pat dry
7. Store in dry bag or container
8. Enjoy!

CAMILLA'S QUESO DIP

Prep Time: 5 min
Cooking time: 10 min

Difficulty: 🎓🎓

Equipment Needed:
Knife for chopping
Small sauté' pot
Lg mixing spoon
Measuring Cup

Ingredients:
½ cup drained salsa
½ cup shredded cheese
1 chopped green onion stalk (optional)

Instructions
1. In sauté pot combine salsa and cheese over low heat,
2. Stir continuously to avoid scorching
3. Top with green onion and enjoy with tortillas

CHESS CLUB CHEESE CUBES

Prep Time: 20 min

Difficulty: 🎓🎓

Equipment Needed:
Small saucepan
Medium mixing bowl
Recycled jar with lid
(Baby jars work great)

Ingredients:
¼ cup sharp cheddar cheese cubes
1/8 cup Olive Oil
½ tablespoon minced sage
1 dash whole peppercorns
Measuring Cup

Instructions
1. In small saucepan combine oil, sage and peppercorn, warm over low heat for 5 minutes
2. Cool mixtures 10 minutes
3. Place cheese in mixing bowl; toss oil mixture over cheese cubes
4. Cover and sit aside for 1 hr. to allow to marinate
5. Transfer cubes from bowl to small jar; garnish with additional sage
6. Enjoy at room temperature with crackers

FIELD DAY FRUIT PIZZA

Prep Time: 10 min
Cooking time: 10 min

Difficulty: 🎓🎓

Equipment Needed:
Small mixing bowl

Ingredients:
*Sugar Free Cookies
½ cup Greek Yogurt
1 teaspoon honey
½ teaspoon vanilla extract
¾ teaspoon orange juice
½ cup sliced & cubed fruit

Instructions

1. Follow the steps for Sugar Free Science Cookie found on page 134 as the base for this recipe
2. In a mixing bowl blend yogurt, honey, vanilla and orange juice
3. Spread yogurt mix over each cookie crust
4. Top with fruit and enjoy!

FIELDTRIP FONDUE

Prep Time: 2 min
Cooking time: 10 min

Difficulty:

Equipment Needed:
Small microwavable Bowl

Toothpicks

Ingredients:
3 ounces semisweet chocolate bar; broken into pieces

2 ounces milk chocolate bar; broken into pieces

¼ cup whole milk

¼ teaspoon pure vanilla

1 tablespoon unsalted butter

Dash sea salt

Dipping Options:
Strawberries

Bananas

Raspberries

Crackers

Instructions
1. Attach pieces of fruit to toothpicks; set aside
2. Microwave chocolates, milk, vanilla, butter and sea salt in bowl for 2-3 minutes (depending on microwave power) DON'T OVERCOOK AND BURN. – If chocolate isn't completely melted stir and microwave for 30 more seconds and repeat as needed
3. Add fondue to warmed thermos
4. Enjoy in warm thermos!

GRADUATE GRANOLA BARS

Prep Time: 5 min
Cooking time: 20 min

Difficulty: 🎓🎓

Equipment Needed:
Medium Mixing Bowl
9x13 Pyrex
Mixing Spoon

Ingredients:
1 ½ cup instant oats
¼ cup cup quinoa
½ cup chopped coconut
½ cup slithered almonds
1 tablespoon melted butter
7 ounces sweetened condensed milk
½ cup miniature semisweet chocolate chips

Instructions
1. Preheat oven to 350 degrees
2. In a medium bowl. Mix together all ingredients
3. Press down into 9x13 pan
4. Bake for 20 minutes
5. Allow 5 minutes to cool before cutting and packing.
6. Enjoy!

JANELLE'S FRUIT JIGGLES

Prep Time: 10 min

Difficulty:

Equipment Needed:
13x9 glass cooking dish
Medium pot
Mixing spoon
Cookie Cutter

Ingredients:
2 cups boiling water
2 packages gelatin (6 oz) mix
1 8 ounce can drained Fruit cocktail

Instructions
1. Spray bottom of glass cooking dish with non-stick cooking spray
2. Add gelatin mix to pot of boiling water, stir until completely dissolved
3. Pour mixture into glass cooking dish
4. Refrigerate for 1 ½ hours
5. Add drained fruit evenly across gelatin
6. Return to refrigerator for an additional 2 hours
7. Dip bottom of glass pan into warm water for 20 sec before cutting with cookie cutter
8. Pack and enjoy chilled!

1-2-3 Lemon Bars

Prep Time: 10 min
Cooking time: 30 min

Difficulty:

Equipment Needed:
Electric Mixer
9 x 13 inch baking pan

Ingredients:
1 box angel food cake mix
21-oz can lemon pie filling

Instructions
1. Mix cake mix and pie filling in electric mixer
2. Bake at 350 0F for 30 minutes, allow to cool
3. Cut into bars and enjoy!

KRISTY'S CRUNCHY APPLE WEDGES

Prep Time: 5 min

Difficulty:

Equipment Needed:
Apple Core or knife
2 Small bowls

Ingredients:
Fresh clean and dried apples
Equal parts water/lemon juice
Almond Butter
1 cup Krispy cereal

Instructions
1. Core apple; cut into wedges
2. In a bowl place wedges immediately into lemon-water mix
3. In a separate bowl add cereal
4. Remove apples from mix and pat dry
5. Spread almond butter to each cut side of apple wedges
6. Roll wedge into cereal bowl
7. Pack in an airtight container for later
8. Enjoy!

MR. MOORE'S MINI CHEESECAKE

Prep Time: 10 min
Cooking time: 20 min

Difficulty:

Equipment Needed:

Hand Mixer

Medium mixing bowl

Cupcake Pan

Cupcake Liners

Rubber Spatula

Ingredients:

Crust:

Crust:

¾ cup Cinnamon Graham Cracker Crumbs

3 tablespoons unsalted butter (melted)

Filling:

½ pack (4oz) cream cheese *room temperature*

1/8 cup sour cream *room temperature*

1 large egg (divided in half)

½ teaspoon vanilla extract

1/8 cup Stevia ™

Instructions

1. Preheat oven to 350 degrees. Line a 6-count muffin pan with cupcake liners (if you are using a 12 count pan – place water in unused cups)
2. CRUST: Hand-mix graham cracker crust with melted butter, divide equally among the 6 cups and press tightly to bottom of cup using a rubber spatula
3. Using hand mixer beat cream cheese until light and fluffy. Add in sour cream, beat for another minute until it too is light and fluffy
4. Add egg, stevia, and vanilla and beat until blended well
5. Divide batter into equal parts, dropping in cups over graham cracker mix.
6. Bake for 18-20 minutes (until mixture begins to brown)
7. Remove from oven and cool completely before refrigerating for 4 hours
8. Enjoy chilled!

MS. RAMIREZ' CHURRO ALMONDS

Prep Time: 10 min
Cooking time: 15 min

Difficulty:

Equipment Needed:
2 medium mixing bowls
Baking Sheet
Parchment paper
Cooking Spray

Ingredients:
1 cup almonds
¼ teaspoon vanilla extract
1/8 cup water
1/8 teaspoon cayenne pepper
Pinch salt
1 tablespoon cinnamon
1/8 cup stevia

Instructions

1. Preheat oven to 350 F
2. Line baking sheet with parchment paper; spray with cooking spray
3. In medium mixing bowl, mix stevia, cinnamon, salt and cayenne
4. In a separate bowl whisk together water and vanilla. Stir in almonds
5. Scoop almonds and mix into dry ingredient bowl until well coated
6. Spread almonds across the baking sheet; bake for 15 mins, stirring occasionally.
7. Cool and store in airtight container
8. Enjoy!

PRESTON'S PB COOKIES

Prep Time: 10 min
Cooking time: 8-10 min

Difficulty: 🎓🎓

Equipment Needed:
Nonstick Cookie Sheet
Mixing Bowl
Large Spoon
Fork
Parchment Paper

Ingredients:
1 cup peanut butter
1 cp Stevia ™
1 large egg

Instructions

1. Preheat oven 325
2. Line your cookie sheet with parchment paper
3. Mix all ingredients together
4. Place a spoonful of batter ½ inch apart on the cookie sheet until you have no batter left in your bowl
5. With a fork, flatten each cookie – creating a crisscross pattern atop
6. Bake 8-10 minutes (Being sure not to overcook)
7. Cool 2-3 mins before packing in an airtight container
8. Enjoy!

RAYLEE'S ROASTED CHICKPEAS

Prep Time: 10 min

Difficulty:

Equipment Needed:
Medium Bowl
Wooden mixing spoon
Parchment Paper

Ingredients:
1 can chickpeas; rinsed & drained
2 tablespoons grated parmesan
1 teaspoon garlic salt
½ tablespoon olive oil

Instructions
1. Preheat oven to 400 F
2. Remove skin from chickpeas by gently pinching
3. Toss in olive oil, parmesan, garlic salt
4. Place on parchment lined cookie sheet; place a single layer on pan
5. Bake for 30-35 minutes until golden brown; toss peas over halfway through baking
6. Enjoy!

Replace parmesan and try one of these flavors
Sesame Soy
Honey Cinnamon
Chili Lime
Ranch
BBQ

RECESS POPCORN BALLS

Prep Time: 10 min

Difficulty:

Equipment Needed:

Disposable Plastic Gloves
3 small bowls
Nonstick Cooking Spray
Parchment Paper
Measuring Cup

Ingredients:

4 oz popped popcorn
Melted Sugar-Free Marshmallows
Food Coloring

Instructions

1. Spray gloves with cooking spray; set aside
2. Place popped popcorn in bowl; set aside
3. Melt sugar-free marshmallow cream; separate into 3 small bowls; add 1 drop of food coloring to each bowl, stir
4. Equally divide popcorn into 3 marshmallow mixtures
5. With gloves on, form small tennis ball portions, packing tightly
6. Store in airtight container
7. Enjoy!

SPOTTED BUTTERFLY BITES

Prep Time: 5 min
Cooking time: 5 min

Difficulty:

Equipment Needed:
Butter Knife
Small bowl

Ingredients:
2 Slices Cinnamon Swirl Bread
2 Tablespoons Cream Cheese; Softened
1 teaspoon sugar-free syrup
1 celery stick, thinly sliced to form curls

Instructions
1. Combine Cream Cheese and syrup into small bowl and mix until syrup is no longer visible
2. Spread mixture onto both bread slices and place cream sides together
3. Stack bread slices: cream sides touching, cut diagonally in both directions creating 2 triangles
4. Build butterfly in a sandwich container

SUGAR-FREE SCIENCE COOKIES

Prep Time: 10 min

Difficulty: 🎓🎓

Equipment Needed:
Hand Mixer

2 medium bowls

Large Spoon

Plastic Wrap

Cutting board

Glass cup

Measuring Spoon

Measuring Cup

Ingredients:
½ cup salted butter softened

¼ cup stevia

1 large egg

1 teaspoon vanilla extract

½ teaspoon baking powder

1 ¼ cup all-purpose flour

Nonstick cooking spray

Instructions

1. Beat Butter & Stevia until fluffy
2. In separate bowl beat egg and vanilla, add to butter mix
3. Add flour and baking powder to mix; blend until dough consistency, roll into a ball
4. Transfer ball of dough into plastic wrap; refrigerate for 30 mins
5. Preheat oven to 350
6. Place refrigerated dough onto floured cutting board; roll dough out to be ¼ thick; use glass to punch dough circles
7. Place cookie dough 2 inches apart on cookie sheet sprayed with non-cook spray. Bake for 10-12 minutes
8. Store in airtight container
9. Enjoy!

*This recipe is used as an ingredient for **Field Day Fruit Pizza**

TEACHER'S TREAT TRAIL MIX

Prep Time: 5 min

Difficulty:

Equipment Needed:
Container with lid
Measuring Cup

Ingredients:
¼ cup Nuts
¼ cup Seeds
¼ cup Dry Fruit
¼ Something Special

Instructions

1. Choose 1 item from each category; nuts, seeds, dry fruit and special ingredient from the list below
2. Place in a container with a lid; shake
   *Want something extra special, consider adding sea salt, cinnamon or nutmeg to your mix and shake well
3. Enjoy!

Nuts	Seeds	Dry Fruit	Special
Almonds	Sunflower	Cranberry	Coconut Flakes
Pecan	Pumpkin	Raisin	Dark Chocolate
Cashew	Hemp	Banana	Pretzels
Peanut	Chia	Apple	Popcorn
Pecan	Flax	Pineapple	Cereal

Winter Break Snowballs

Prep Time: 20 min

Difficulty: 🎓🎓

Equipment Needed:

Medium bowl
Melon Baller
Measuring Cup
Parchment Paper

Ingredients:

4 ounces cream cheese – softened
1 teaspoon coconut extract
¼ cup natural sweetener (whole earth)
¼ cup unsweetened coconut flakes

Instructions

1. In a bowl mix cream cheese, whole earth and coconut extract
2. Lay parchment paper out, sprinkle coconut flakes atop
3. Use melon baller to scoop cream cheese mix; roll the balls in coconut flakes
4. Chill overnight before packing for lunch
5. Enjoy in chilled thermos!

ZIHYON'S ZUCCHINI MUFFINS

Prep Time: 5 min
Cooking time: 20 min

Difficulty: 🎓🎓🎓

Equipment Needed:
Bowl
Mixing Spoon
Cupcake holder
Muffin Pan

Ingredients:
½ cup drained, shaved zucchini
½ tablespoon honey
½ cup flour
½ teaspoon pure vanilla extract
1/3 cup almond butter
2 eggs
½ teaspoon baking powder
½ teaspoon cinnamon
¼ cup slithered walnuts

Instructions
1. Preheat oven to 350F
2. In bowl combine all ingredients
3. Fill each cupcake holder ¾ full
4. Bake for 18-20 minutes
5. Cool muffins before serving
6. Enjoy!

TINK'S TABLE

Let's Talk!

I want to know your favorite recipe. What recipe was the messiest, the most challenging? Send your thoughts to tinks.healthy.kitchen@gmail.com

I hope you've had the chance to try many different lunch combinations and have found your favorite! I would love to hear from you.

Make your favorite dish and send us a picture! It just might be featured on social media!
Use #tinkshealthykitchen or @tinkshealthykitchen to connect with us.

Send photos to: tinkshealthykitchen@gmail.com

WANT MORE FOOD FUN? TRY THESE RECIPES!

EDIBLE JELLO™ SLIME

Prep Time: 5 min

Difficulty: 👨‍🍳👨‍🍳👨‍🍳

Equipment Needed:

Medium mixing bowl
Mixing spoon
Parchment Paper

Ingredients:

1 cup cornstarch
1 lg box (6 ounces) Sugar-Free Jello
Warm Water

Instructions

1. In mixing bowl combine cornstarch and sugar free gelatin.
2. Add ½ cup warm water; mix well until color begins forming.
3. Add 2 Tsp water and mix.
4. Repeat steps 3 until slime begins to form a paste – do not dump remaining water as you may not need it all.

*Step 4 is very important, too much water will cause a sticky mess!

AFTERSCHOOL SNACK

Tomatoes (Cherry)
Infused Water (Strawberry & Mint)
Nectarine Wedges
Kiwi Halves

FOOD JOKE ANSWERS

1. Lettuce in and you'll see.
2. Because it saw the salad dressing.
3. Cashews
4. Ketchup!
5. An impasta
6. A box of quakers!
7. His teacher told him it was a piece of cake.
8. Waiter: "No it's going to be round"
9. Launch Meat
10. Close the door, I'm dressing.
11. A Chew E Bar
12. Pears
13. A meatball
14. We're friends because we're both nuts
15. Tater Tots
16. Because his mom told him it was chili outside.
17. Root Beer
18. A Teapot
19. To make ends meat.
20. He was on a roll.
21. When you are eating a watermelon
22. Bleu Cheese
23. A jam session
24. Wow, I relish the fact that you've mustard the strength to ketchup to me.
25. They were in mint condition.
26. Pulled Pork
27. It was an Oscar Wiener
28. A boiled egg
29. Even the cake was in tiers
30. Because he gave her 10 carrots.

INDEX

- 7 STEPS TO GET A GRADE A IN THE KITCHEN
- Apple; Apple Snail, Apple Donuts, Apple Wedge
- Almond Butter; Apple Donut, Apple Wedge, Zucchini Muffin
- Avocado, Guacamole
- ACKNOWLEDGEMENTS
- Bacon; Bacon Brussels; Cheese and Bacon Rolls, Loaded Potato
- Bananas; Dolp-fun Snack Bowl, Banana Sushi
- Bars; Granola Bars
- Beans; Beans and Rice, Chili
- Beef; Chili, Traveling Nachos
- Bell Peppers: Safety Pepper, Monster Cup
- Bread; Cookie Cutter Sandwich, Cheese and Bacon Roll, Math Sandwich Sticks; Butterfly Bites, Burgers, Salad on Stick, Brushetta, Butterfly Bites
- Broccoli; Loaded Potato, Cauli-Rice
- Brussel Sprouts; Bacon Brussels
- Carrott; Salad Cup
- Cauliflower; Cauli Popcorn; Cauli-Rice
- Celery; Seafood Salad, Chicken Wrap, Apple Snail, Apple Donut, Zoodle Soup, Butterfly Bites
- Cilantro; Guacamole
- Cheese ; Bacon Roll, Pizza, Quesadilla, Mac and Cheese, Cookie Cutter Sandwich, Egg Muffin, Cheese Chips, Roasted Chickpeas, Queso Dip, Cheese Cubes, Loaded Potato, Traveling Nachos
- Chicken; Pinwheel, Waffle Stick, Zoodle Soup
- Chick Peas; Hummas, Roasted Chickpeas
- Chili & Soup; Cafeteria Chili, Beans and Rice, Chicken Zoodle Soup
- Chocolate; Bus Stop Bacon, Granola Bars, Fondue
- Coconut; Snowballs, Granola Bars
- Cucumber; Salad Cup, Cucumber Chips,
- Cream Cheese; Taco Dip, Safety Peppers, Spinach Dip, Snowballs, Cheesecake, Butterfly Bites
- DEDICATIONS
- Eggs; Egg Muffin, PB Cookies, Cheesecake, Science Cookies
- FOOD GROUPS
- FOOD JOKE ANSWERS
- FOOD JOKES
- Fruit; Fruit Wand, Dolp-fun Snack Bowl, Melon Pops, Flower Cup, Orange Snail, Fruit Pizza, Granola Bars, Fondue
- Garlic; Cauli-Rice, Chili, Beans and Rice; Guacamole
- Gelatin; Fruit Jiggles
- Hazlent; Banana Sushi
- Honey; Zucchini Muffin, Fruit Pizza
- Jams & Jelly
- KITCHEN FUNDAMENTALS
- KITCHEN TOOLS
- KNIFE SAFETY
- Lemon; lemon squares
- Lettuce; Chicken Wrap, Salad Cup, Salad on Stick, Traveling Nachos
- Marshmallows; Popcorn Balls
- Mayo; Seafood Salad, Chicken Wrap
- Milk; Mac and Cheese, Egg Muffin, Granola Bars, Fried Green Tomatoes, Fodue
- MEASURING CHEAT SHEET
- MOM AND DAUGHTER BIO
- Muffins; egg Muffin, Zucchini Muffin
- Noodles & Pasta; Seafood Salad, Perfect Pasta
- Nuts; Zucchini Muffin, Trail Mix, Churro Almonds, Granola Bars
- Onion: beans and Rice, Perfect Pasta, Chili, Salad Cup, Guacamole, Egg Muffin, Salad on Stick
- Orange; Snail
- PACKING YOUR BEST LUNCH IN A THERMOS
- Pasta; Seafood Salad, Perfect Pasta
- Peanut Butter; Hummas, Banana Sushi, Apple Snail, PB Cookies
- Peppers; Perfect Pasta
- Pizza; Valentine's Day Pizza
- Popcorn; Popcorn Balls
- Potatoes & Sweet Potatoes; Sweet Potato Crisp, Loaded Potato
- Prepared Dough; Pizza
- Rice; Beans and Rice, Cauli-Rice
- Salad; Archery Salad Cup, Salad on a Stick, Seafood Salad
- Sanwiches & Wraps; Chicken Wrap, Math Sandwiches, Pinwheels, Butterfly Bites
- Sauages; Beans and Rice
- Shrimp; Seafood Salad
- Sour Cream; Taco Dip, Spinach Dip, Cheesecake, Loaded Potato
- SPECIAL THANKS
- Spinach; Egg Muffin, Spinach Dip
- Tacos; Taco Dip
- TINK'S TABLE
- Tomatoes; Perfect Pasta, Chicken Wrap, Chili, Salad Cup, Guacamole, Salad on Stick, Bruschetta, Traveling Nachos, Fried Green Tomatoes
- Tortillas; Chicken Wrap, Quesadilla, Banana Sushi
- Turkey; Chili, Burgers, Queso Dip
- UNDERSTANDING COOKBOOK LEVEL SYMBOLS
- Wraps; Chicken Wrap, Pin Wheels
- Yogurt; , Fruit Pizza
- Zucchini; Cauli-Rice, Zucchini Muffin, Zoodle Soup

www.ingramcontent.com/pod-product-compliance
Lightning Source LLC
Chambersburg PA
CBHW040757240426
43673CB000014B/365